LAST
HOURS

LAST
HOURS

jennifer may newhook

Riddle Fence Debuts
St. John's, NL

LAST HOURS
Copyright © 2024 by Jennifer May Newhook

Riddle Fence Publishing Inc.
PO Box 7092
St. John's, NL A1E 3Y3, Canada
www.riddlefence.com

The publisher gratefully acknowledges the support of the Canada Council for the Arts, the Newfoundland and Labrador Arts Council, and the Government of NL.

Riddle Fence Publishing acknowledges the land on which we work as the ancestral homelands of the Beothuk, whose culture has now been erased forever. We also acknowledge the island of Ktaqmkuk (Newfoundland) as the unceded, traditional territory of the Beothuk and the Mi'kmaq. And we acknowledge Labrador as the traditional and ancestral homelands of the Innu of Nitassinan, the Inuit of Nunatsiavut, and the Inuit of NunatuKavut.

Cover and text design by: Graham Blair
Cover art by: Hollie Chastain, "Found Her Voice"
Edited by: Sue Goyette

Printed and bound in Canada

Library and Archives Canada Cataloguing in Publication
Title: Last hours / Jennifer May Newhook.
Names: Newhook, Jennifer May, author.
Description: Poems.
Identifiers: Canadiana (print) 20230590675 | Canadiana (ebook) 20230590721 | ISBN 9781738151523 (softcover) | ISBN 9781738151530 (HTML)
Subjects: LCGFT: Poetry.
Classification: LCC PS8627.E8648 L37 2024 | DDC C811/.6—dc23

For my family—all of whom are present here.

Contents

i.

Ornery Corner

On the ornery corner of Aldershot n Summer
stray dogs barked n shat tattered cats
fought n spat—in the middle of Rabbittown
buddy thats where it all went down—
on the sticky sidewalks gummed grey
in layers where beer bottles smashed
n garbage blew everywhere except the trash
in the nights—thats when teens in knots
gathered tight round broke-down cars
n souped-up trucks all long hair wide legs
bad skin every transistor in town
tuned loud to OZFM.

At the end of the broken sidewalk
across from the big purple lilac
there was a tiny n strange-angled fish shop
run by Jimmys mother Missus Badcock
where for one whole spring a crow with a broken wing
cawed from a cardboard box right there
on the countertop next to fresh cod fillet
tongues n cheeks buckets of fatback n salt beef
hand-knit mittens a brace of rabbits sacks of spuds
n tubs of bakeapple—stinkin all of it
like Juicy Fruit n guts cigarette butts n fish—
in the case of the crow all covered in shit.

Merrymeeting Laundromat spat out suds
n the rummies lurched up from the burnt-down
Cottage Club pissed their pants n then passed out
n every single day the Umma Mumma Man
trudged up Mayor all the way from Churchill Square
dragged his built-up boot n at the top laid down
his shoeshine box noddin n winkin limpin n mumblin
umma mumma umma mumma to the beat-down bums
n the snot-nosed kids—some threw rocks n
some waved back—like old Johnny Gluebag
I hear they still sleeps it off in the tire tracks
on the ornery corner of Aldershot n Summer.

O Wanda Whalen

O Wanda,
where are you?

You unspoken queen
of the Grade Five classroom;
your face is in front of me
as clear as my own mother's.
Hair, dark brown—chopped
hard like Joan Jett, feathered
soft like a Cassidy—you sat
just ahead and to my left
for almost a whole year,
the one you probably
should have spent in
Grade Seven.

Eyes blue,
hard-lined black—

the only girl in the fifth grade
with a leather purse, a Mötley Crüe
T-shirt, a full deck of smokes,
a matching set of double D breasts,
and the 24-pack of smelly markers.
I was scared of you, as I stared
at your boobs for nearly a full year,
but you weren't mean, at least
not to me. Not like Roxanne
with the grey front tooth, or Gina,
who went on to sell real estate
with a turned-up collar. You
disappeared partway through
the year and you never came back
visibly pregnant like Lorna and Alison,
or with a job like DeForest.

O Wanda,
I could write odes

to you and your acid-washed
jeans, your North Star sneakers,
and your frosted pink lipstick,
your cola Lip Smackers, juicy rollers,
and all of your scratch and sniff stickers.

Wanda, I must confess—
I think I really wanted

you to be my babysitter.
Just the two of us, on one of your Nan's
satin-edged blankets, in your tiny
backyard on the Blocks or in the Circle
or on the Courts; our Harlequins tented,
Coppertone SPF 3 on the summer breeze,
OZFM asking us over and over,
Who are you . . . Who are you?

O Wanda Whalen . . .
I wish it was
still just you
and me.

With the Lights On

Our first order of business—
nominate a Spirit Whisperer.
One to call out the imprecise gloom
for those sad, strayed, and catastrophically
unbodied to join us in our giggling,

gum-chewing, corporeal glee. In the dark,
listen tensely for the thumps and bangs
and moans requested as proof of presence; fall
apart into gales at the inevitable, anonymous,
and exuberant fart. Feral, reckless—

we teeter briefly on Death's doorstep,
our collective breath spurring some furtive
transmutation—from silly seance to grave
flirtation—the spun bottle, glass-thin,
wracks our nervous circle.

Uncertain, due to the tensely
anticipated summoning, the slippery
and slightly repulsive kisses following—
which teenage ghost it actually was
that made each one of us sleep that night

with the lights on.

ii.

Morning in the Cauldron

Yesterday's trees were crosses.
Today, thousands of small hands
unfold ten thousand fans—
it's the rain that brings out the praying;
this view will be gone by tomorrow at noon.

Signal Hill, the Southside,
and the City of St. John's—
that sagging amphitheatre of steaming, canted,
mansard roofs, stepping and leaning and tumbling
the steep, downtown slope
to the water.

Don't pray
for this poor man's coliseum,
the centuries of sad, Victorian shades,
the flaking marine paint.

This cauldron
is full up with cigarette butts and cars on blocks—
hidden by trees and their greedy leaves, palms open wide
in benediction as new grass raises up, old fences splay out,
and small birds rain down
on the coal black dirt.

Come to your feet
with the sudden, hard Atlantic gust
that forces the trees to bow all to the ground
and every flag to stand up and clap;

rise, in a standing O
for the goutweed that grows
over bits of broken china and years of smashed
glass, winking in the grass.

Put your hands together
in rapturous—no, *thunderous*—applause
for each solitary sharp-shinned hawk and feral cat
that stalks the knotweed
for fledgling chicks
and rats among the rocks.

Give a big hand
for every street downtown,
rank from Saturday night;

shout loud praise
for the pools of hotdog vomit
and the condom slops.

Raise a glass
to cheer each broken bottle, dirty needle,
and spanworm moth that scatters the sidewalk
from the Cauldron to the Southside,
Signal Hill to
Amherst Rock.

Re: Muskrat Falls

(cc: Ball, Bennett, Furey, et al.)

This is
cross-generational,
moratorium-level
fuckery,
and it has to stop.

You want to come at me
motherfuckers—
Ball, Bennett, Furey, et al.?

We came of age
as the fishery collapsed.
We came of age,
raised on CBC and NTV,
watching poor old men
from the bay
trying to beat down
the closed doors
of closed meetings
with folding chairs.

We came of age
when the *Estai* was dragged
into port—for stealing
what was left
of the undersized fish.

We gathered, silent,
on that fenceless harbourfront,
a crowd of a thousand,
to watch those piss-poor pescadores
walk the plank, while you—
the true architects of our distress,
sat behind your desks.

We threw a single fucking egg.

Speaking of angry,
we've watched fish plants
and boat factories burn.
We've seen families leave,
whole towns turn ghost,
punts on slips grow grass,
and government wharves collapse;
inshore folk, completely broke,
leaving their homes, turning in tags,
and selling their boats.

Lineups—a block long
for a single job
at the local gas station,
while some fuckers'
factory freezers float
just off the Grand Banks,
vacuuming entire ecosystems
into building-sized boats.

Come at me, motherfuckers—
that summer there *was* no summer.

We graduated high school
as every rat fled the sinking ship,
compound interest mounting
on every defaulted student loan.

For our own good,
the narrative—
what else did we expect?
Have-not, butt-end, pogey-draining
welfare-cases, the lot,
said the mainland papers.

Motherfuckers, *you* did it—
pocketed your share of our money
when they crossed the 200-mile limit—

and you're doing it again,
you oil-shilling, condo-selling,
franchise-owning, library-closing,
book-taxing, crony-backing,
cock-knocking
sons of bitches.

The fog is lifting—
you better watch out.

Bigger Fish

There's people
tryna make a living
tryna feed their families
ya know.

We got bigger fish
to fry so shut yer
garbage hole. Go preen
yer feathers elsewhere—

we got a cold house
this morning and
the Frosted Flakes box
is bout empty.

I aint got no problem
with wimmen just only
yer big mouth so
shut yer art hole

fer the love of fuck—
no one understands
yer stupid plain
face. Three months

behind now on the rent
and some fucken hippy
snowflake is flappin her jaw
all over the interweb—

that club pack of frozen
fries got to last out
the month and heres me
yellin at the kids

Stop eatin them friggen
frozen french fries!
And you cant shut
yer trap even one minute

bout someone talkin
bout grabbin someone
elses pussy—Jesus
Christ heres the gun.

Were gonna have to
go out for a moose.
If you got time to
whine about pussy

heres the knife—stick it
up the arse and slice right
through the middle. See
if you got time now—

with all of them guts
fallin out and blood
and shit sometimes too—
to think about some

art thing or some goddamn
welfare thing. Never stop
talkin—sick to death
of the old garbage fallin

out yer garbage hole
every second. Theres
a roof needs tarrin
kids room got a leak.

Cant no one afford to get sick
now—Junior in there shoulda
had glasses these three years
Susie needs her tooth pulled

and you cant shut up
bout yer goddamn pussy!
I don't give a fuck about
your hairy old hole—

I got bigger fish to fry.

Last Hours, in Port

The *Lyubov Orlova*
is finally keeling over.

Gangplank askew,
hung crooked by ropes—
the rats have this boat
by the throat.

She's been tagged
on the bow
by a bad graffiti artist.

Her bilges
have been
breached.

The *Orlova* once
ran aground
at Deception Island.

She is also Lyubov 3108,
a minor planet
sailing the outer
reaches of space.

She is still
the most famous
actress under Stalin,

understand,
she has fallen
on hard times.

See her lean
into the apron,
a tired Russian matron

taking on water
in the City of Legends.

Last Hours, at Sea

The *Orlova*'s rescue beacons
    broadcast . . . distress.
  Set deliberately – – – adrift
        sinking . . . by inches
        she lists
      in the cold night wind,
thick skin blistered . . . by multiple hematomas,
    ferrous papilloma – – – yawing indecently,
      her rusty gunwales . . . tip
        as she slowly   slips
           under.
  Far down
        her narrow   nautical pass

she is still rolled out . . . with red carpet,

    decked by – – – autographed photographs,

   a tilted movie still . . . a stage bouquet
   of silk flowers,

        mildewed.

Deep

    in the derelict hold,

          low

  in the bloated bilge,

      her final audience   . . .   floats.

   Rats,   a full house.

          All belly up.

   Each tiny   – – –

          cannibal hand,

in applause   . . .
        upturned.

Last Hours, on Stage

Moya Lyubov,
you hid from the sun
in the days and weeks and years
after your first husband was stolen
by Stalin. Taken, how often in those times,
at night, in silence. Without explanation.
Andrei disappeared, deep into
the gulag. Your star rose high
under movie lights,
bright and
long and

lonely.

General Secretary
Stalin, in 1934, declared
you "The Most Famous Actress
Under Stalin." By then, your first husband
had no star. Andrei grew thin under the no-moon,
forgotten by everyone and his wife. Joseph, one day,
offered a gift. Anything at all. You asked, in secret, to meet
with your stolen spouse. Taken off guard, Stalin suggested
that if you wanted to see him so badly, you could
live with Andrei and the rats in the gulag.
You found your first
husband

diminished.

The pieces
taken in every
interrogation had not
grown back in the right order
or place. You turned your back
on Andrei. Some years later,
he walked out of the gulag,
into another life,
and

died.

Lyubov.
After this visit,
you were so sensitive,
to the sun and the moon
and lights. To your second
husband's chagrin—
you drank too
much and
grew

old.

After Picasso
(or was it Charlie Chaplin)
bought your new, American face,
you wore long gloves to hide your aging
hands. You slept the days away and drifted out
each night, restless; buoyed by pills
and the right dress. You didn't
hear the scattered applause.
You never saw them
rise to their feet
as you

sank.

Goodnight Moon

(for Margaret Wise Brown
and Michael Strange)

Dearest Blanche,
Michael, Sir Baby,
my most cherished Rabbit . . .

So late,
you've sent
me away. Alone
at the Only House,
I watch the clouds
moving over, like
they do in
movies.

The dark
sky here is burnt
orange. Thin cries skim
the ocean, night gulls
are high and
white.

Far below,
bones roll over
with the sea spiders
and brittle stars
that prickle
the black
trench.

We are
bottom feeders,
you and I (though
we pretend otherwise),
our avid feelers meant
to probe freezing depths
for floating motes
and necrotic
flesh . . .

our quivering bits
to bioluminesce.

Whales sleep,
great and silent,
suspended in this deep.
Here, where now
is always
our last
breath.

Shhh . . .

There are other bodies here,
in the great grey room.

Ghost
ships adrift,
slip their knots,
sink by inches. Slowly,
gently, rock their
corpses.

Between us
(can you feel it?)
every feather vibrates
with our first gasp and
that last push. With
the coming final
bloodless
gush.

Goodnight nobody,
goodnight mush.

Dear Margaret—

I've asked you
not to write.

Though,
I have heard,
far north, ancient men
and archaic animals
are surfacing, half-
eaten, from
Stone Age
dirt.

Carcasses
like boiled pigs,
half-baked, frost-
burnt, have swum
up from
tundra.

Like
your awful
wolf-skin jacket,
they shed clumps
of rust-coloured hair,
flags of jerk-brown
skin, stone tools,
tusks, and
teeth.

We too
have sewn
the story of
the leather man.
Our tiny stitches were
made with small
eyes, and now
it seems the
seams have
burst.

I've shrunk
since we last met;
my limbs have grown
painfully thin, and I'd hate
for you to see them. Think
instead of my sharp
blazers on stage,
ablaze!

Before bed,
I made the mistake
of reading the good
book. Later, I pulled
up our old, familiar sod
to sleep and found it
threadbare . . .

goodnight is always soon.

Across
the long hallway,
my golden wishbone
still winks at your throat;
the flowers you left
behind are nothing
but sticks.

There is no light, no red balloon.

We can
only drag
(alone, my dear)
to the edge of
that dark water
and drink.

Last of the Lilacs

Laburnum, lilac, blue flag iris, lupins,
monkshood, foxglove digitalis, fireweed,
forget-me-nots, and Rosa acicularis—
all erupt in the fiery, golden haze

that has hung over the Avalon for weeks.
Incendiary, blooms detonate among leaves
that are slick with the uncommon gloss
of hot sun and the usual heavy rain;

the air exhales colour and smoke.
Everywhere, in every emerald lane,
carmine clematis pinwheels spin,
and starry asters wheel. Salvia divinorum,

allium, and pink, bouffant peonies explode
over lapped olive and turquoise clapboard; golden
chains hang molten from the branches. Dripping
to the dirt, Laburnum alpinum ignites

Papaver somniferum; swollen opium poppies
that burst suddenly, like orange
underskirts, from overstuffed, silvery
suitcases. The long rays and banked-coal

blaze of a lingering wildfire sunset singes
the last of the lilacs. Syringa vulgaris skulks
the shadows, intoxicated, dropping her bruised
blooms like used tissues on the perfumed pavement.

iv.

Titans

In the final hours
of my first pregnancy,
the bloody waters
broke. Pain breached
through dark waves.

I tried to find a place
that was safe
because there was a giant.
It had a ragged cloak
that was made of dead

seaweed. It's dry, alive
fingers grew rootlike
into the narrow, dripping
crevasse where I hid;
its brittle joints, by feel,
trying to find any crack.

Finally, a needle pierced
epidural space. I slipped
under the dark weight
of water-heavy clouds.
Later, I crawled out

into the fog as the giant
strode off, smashing rotten
sheds with boulder fists,
with legs like tree trunks,
that went up and disappeared.

Painful spines sank
back into deep water.
I found a place,
a rocky shore.
Like all women,
laboured alone.

Titan is lost,
under uncountable
acres of Atlantic Ocean . . .
Did any of those men
ever run, gravid,
from war?

Did they ever stumble?
Clenched, contracting,
and desperate to keep
their combined blood
from staining the grass.

The Hours It Takes

I felt it fly from me.
I mean, I actually saw it go.
Me and the one other woman
in the grocery store parking lot.

The two of us, watching
the bright foil balloon
she had just bought
slip the knot,

and sail over downtown
for the Narrows, trailing
ribbons, quickly dwindling
in the glow of the setting sun.

It is gone.
The gonest thing that ever was.

In my skirt, at the edge
of the parking lot, I am
clutching a bottle of newly
purchased prenatal vitamins.

The other woman stands
as still as me. We are each
our own statues, separated
by the sparkling sea of parked cars.

Together, watching the balloon
become smaller and higher,
more distant, and less
of anything at all.

I am 41 years old. This is my fourth
bottle of such vitamins in ten years.

My youngest son, weeks before,
on his fourth birthday, watched
the blue balloon I'd blown for him
in celebration escape his grasp,

bounce and tumble and blow
down over the long drung, up
into the blue sky, out over the blue
ocean, and into Grates Cove far below.

He lay down in the blowing,
unmowed grass and howled.

Me, I watch that woman's
balloon disappear from view—
they both leave with the sun.
I take my vitamins.

I look down at my feet,
still in their party shoes.
I clock the thousand steps,
the running jump,

the many feathers grown
from force of will,
the agony of bony wings
burst from shoulder blades.

The hours of flight required
to catch a lost balloon.

Spring Is in the Gut

(a meditation on unplanned pregnancy at advanced maternal age, with brass band)

The lake
is doused in fog—
the far end of her, lost.
Blurred shores all
snow melt and garbage wash
where paired ducks pick
through moldy detritus,
enjoying their coupled bliss—
as yet, duckling-less.
Gulls brood the wet, brown hill;
gulls bob the grey lake,
the gulls are one
mournful, seaside cry,
each mouthful a complaint—
one on top of the other
and the other.

Pondside,
lost mitts bloom—
fat, unmatched woolen
birds hung in low
tree branches. One
underwater, unfortunate,
all gull-unstrung
and long unravelling.
Red, like guts.
Down past the slaughter
house, where shift
workers sluice blood
from factory floors,
industrial smoke uncurls,
long, over the pinched
gut's breakwater.

Dam still, and water,
glass. In a thicket of mist
where sky is water,
and water, sky—
a lone rower floats.
Her racing shell
is as narrow
as an airplane's wing.
It cleaves the glass lake.
With each oar dipped,
the fog lifts a bit,
and in it, far distant,
some sort of booming
hurdy-gurdy is unfurling;
a kind of creaking calliope
starts turning.

Under the uneasy rumble
of horses or thunder—
maybe guns—abrupt,
when the cacophony erupts.
A sudden battery of fife
and drum thumps into bloom,
and *ta da!*
Like a lady from a cake,
a brass band bursts
exuberantly from the flume
on the far, more pleasant
side of the lake. The parade
blossoms in the haze—
red as an acre
of Fusilier tulips turning
their heads to the sun.

Metronomic, improbable,
this barrage of tom-tom
and timpani; the erratic splatter
of cymbal and gong. Big top
and bellicose are the mello
and sousaphones, the flugelhorn
and double bell euphonium—
a wonderful grand band
baying into the fog.
Barking snares tree
the tambourines; the glockenspiel's
chimes outfox the triangles'
ring-a-ling collars
and *tally ho!*
This Barnum & Bailey
cannonade is away.

The cavalcade retreats,
leaving its heartbeat—
a disintegrating melody,
gone to ground in the murk.
Those hanging notes ghost
the watchtower. They catch
on the barbed-wire walls
of the penitentiary, linger
in the moss, soft on every weathered
stone in the cemetery.
They whisper past winding paths
that hug the cribbed graves
of children, twisting up the hill
to where the beautiful old
blowjob tree used to be.

A beech tree—so large
and carved with chipped
initials and hieroglyphs—
it was thicker around
than two sets of arms
could reach. Near that naked,
rough, and stumped spot,
a quiet gloaming glints
on glass. Arch, it winks
betwixt the monoliths,
among the headstones
and the cenotaphs;
revealing, most lasciviously,
that the hoary trunks
of the grave old maples
have been tapped.

Hanging from spouts,
clear sap overflows
the mason jars' mouths.
Everywhere, sugary syrup
glistens the ruched bark
and boles and thick
shafts; on every side
it drools from the spiles
right down to
the gnarly roots that clutch
the graves, that grab
the ground, and shake
it with giant hands—
trembling the tight,
green buds, bursting
at the crown.

Across the lake,
the last echoes of the horns'
bright flourish diminish.
The steady, dwindling beat
of the drum major's mace,
laced by thin, ringing bells,
slips through the clearing
fog—a clarion call,
descending. Ground bound
gulls clap suddenly
skyward, a lone racing
shell sculls for the slip,
small mittens bloom
fat in the greening
trees, and spring
is in the Gut.

Atwood Machine

(for Ivy and I)

i.

It was
the summer
of flowers. Fibonacci
spirals sprang from
every branch and
limb's crease.
A season
of strawberries
grown fat and shiny,
raspberries, plump and
dusty, plentiful among
thorn-laced canes.
Trees bent,
hunched
by the weight
of early cherries.
Twisted branches bristled
with hard, green apples,
to the exclusion
of leaves.
Every single
field for miles:
reduced, to the
simple formula
for pie.

i.

Evidently,
I am not exempt.
Sitting on the splintered
front step in frayed

pajama pants, I am
the vacuum of space.
On the bathroom counter
two floors above,
a dripping piss-stick
confirms this reality:
I am knocked up
with my fourth
child.

My
uterus,
a torus
folding
in on itself.
Somewhere,
a map that
describes it.
I am too old
for this.
I have been
made weak,
feeble from
constructing
too many crust-
less sandwiches.
From changing an
infinity of shitty
diapers.

ii.

This
profusion
of strawberries
is confusing.
They linger stupidly

late into the season,
become overgrown with
raspberries and currants
that ripen ridiculously
early, at the unorthodox
end of July. Outside
the city, thick mats
of partridge, crow,
and blueberry
are insistent;
they tangle
every inch
of the barrens.
The tart,
wild scent
contained in even
one raw berry,
ripening
in a single
small bush,
hidden
in a vast
field of rock,
predicts darkly—
accurately—a harvest
so heavy, so unheard of,
it will border on
Higgsian.

iii.

The sun
slams down.
My three boys
caper in the vast
summer heat,
demanding

swimming,
picnics, a pocket
knife, a popsicle,
a game of hide-
and-seek.
My ears
still ring from
the bomb blast, or
more accurately, if
you were to consult a
physicist, the event
that occurs when
two opposing
particle beams
collide.
Covered
in dust, one
pant leg torn off,
I am seated somewhere.
Anywhere. Nowhere. Null,
void, blank from shock.
It is in this state—
a picture once
published in some
foreign country's news-
paper, as a set of raw data
collected but impossible
to analyze with current
mathematical models—
I contemplate my options.
I see you, blastocyte.
Nobbled little bakeapple,
implanted in my literal flesh.
Corded and floating
in the growing
inland sea.
There,

the dots
of spinal cord
as the torus folds
the neural tube.
Here,
the spots
for eyes and
the fishy little
tail. Sibling
to my other
three.

v.

Due to a
momentary lapse
in reproductive vigilance,
I have been captured. Made
the subject of a cruel lab
experiment conducted
eternally in some
vast and circular
machine.
Personally,
I verify every
mechanical law
of motion: wild-eyed,
foam-flecked, vomit-specked.
I cannot survive this unnatural
and constant acceleration; for
God's sake, I am *old*. I will be
quartering grapes well into my
second quadranscentennial—
the obvious and simple
solution: stillness.
Complete
cessation

of the oscillation.
Termination of
acceleration.
Amplitude
death.

viii.

The list is short:
September 4th, 10:45 a.m.
Light breakfast, bath, or shower,
clean shirt, underpants, socks.
My wrinkled belly, well-used,
smooths as the uterine bag
fills with the inner
amniotic sea.
I tell myself
it is only
an old, folded
purse, overstuffed
with crumpled tissue,
used ChapSticks, Tums . . .
Outside the bedroom window,
our elderly city is elaborately fertile,
an equation of state so bountiful
as to astound even the most
austere townie native.
Nothing sensible
I can think of
takes this into
account.
The infinite
series loops end-
lessly: long days of
sunlight, short nights
of summer rain, and
suddenly, the most

vacant and garbage-
stricken of lots
is groaning
with
growth.
In this amaze-
ment of birdsong
and honeybees, I am
a single node. One
solitary particle,
accelerating.

xiii

There is a map:
one hundred years old,
brittle, and foxed, plotted by
Poincaré—in which the torus is
impossible to apprehend simply.
Linear theory and logistic maps
no longer apply. We can attempt
only to examine closely what
flows through the subspace.
That which disappears
or appears
only in the moment
in which it is observed.
There are the simple sums
of pollinators: the effects of
butterflies, the busy work
of bees, but to sense the
golden hush, the haze
settling over this
senior city
is to see
inevitable
and complicated

patterns emerge in the
chaotic lace and regular
dust sets of Julia and Fatou.
We all feel the effects of Noah
(sudden discontinuous change can occur)
and Joseph
(persistence of a value can occur for a while and then suddenly change).
It is
evident
that this is
a summer of
astonishing fertility.
It is also clear that the
crooked buildings, the
stately churches,
will
continue their
elaborate decay.
That I, approaching
the end of my own
bloom, apparently,
am theoretically
still fecund.

iv.

You.
You are
here and/or,
you are not
here.
The
ultimate
quintessence.
The smallest unit
into which matter
can be divided, a

question mark
on the newly
revised
periodic
table of
' elements.
A completely
hypothetical form
of darkest energy,
you confirm
every
observation
of the accelerating
rate of the expanding
known and unknown
universe. Between us,
we demonstrate the
dynamics of the
free fall
apparatus:
you are the
weight, I am
the vertical
scale that
shows
the
distance
of the
fall.

Potential.

Disambiguation.

Interference.

Coherence.

Words

that lose

all meaning

when

the

double

pendulum

starts

to

swing

v.

Celestial Bodies

The moon came up
like a half-peeled orange
over the sea—
started a racket
in the back seat
of the pickup truck.
It's a blood moon.
No, it's called a pirate moon!
That there's a rogue
moon, boys.
We always called it
a harvest moon
and when it rises
all the way up,
it will look just
like a boiled egg,
three-quarters like that.

The three boys
are belted across
the bench seat in back.
Our small daughter
exudes an umber,
infant glow, leaning
between us, asleep.
Planetary in slumber,
infant gravity grounds
us, until (in the middle
of nowhere, or maybe
over Ochre Pit Cove)
a sharp burst
of fireworks explodes—
allium, asters, zinnia,
and cosmos spatter
the black sky,

turning the rusty
old truck roller coaster,
hurtling us on busted
struts, through twisted
backroads, over potholes
and ruts—the rear-view
gone funhouse mirror,
kids howling feral,
carny thrill, world turning
Cyclone,
Tilt-A-Whirl.
Through the cracked
windshield, we are sprinkled
with sparkling sparks,
and we drink, laughing—
dripping blood moon
juice—until everyone

is bursting to pee.
So, we haul the truck
over into the black
and the brush.
The three boys tumble
out in a clump, stand
side by side by side
at the edge of the ditch,
and I never was
so proud in my life, seeing
them shoulder to shoulder
to shoulder, under the orange,
old, and unblinking
eye of the moon—
laughing at the black
sky. Pissing rivers
into the abyss.

Family Problem

We were infected
by some nightmare
germ that turned us
from family
into feral hunters
of each other.

Your father and me,
we were bitten
first. We knew
it was only a matter
of time before the hunger
took over.

So we decided
to solve the problem.
Instead of us eating you
or you eating us,
we'd put you
to sleep.

We relieved
the local pharmacy
of enough phenobarbital
to dose us all.
We crushed up
one hundred pills,

stirred them into
bowls of ice cream.
We fed it to you kids.
You lapped it all up
with lengthening tongues
and pointed teeth.

Then, your father and
me, we each swallowed
and swallowed a thousand,
thousand more pills and
prayed, stomachs growling,
to fall asleep first.

Selene Sees the Moon

The cry comes—
youngest of fifty.

I ascend,
just behind the shadow.
Pour a glass
of water; daughter
twenty-six drinks
standing in the crib
beside our bed.
I pick her up
—the thought,
as long legs,
strong and brown
from summer, wrap
around my waist
—the thought,
as small arms
tighten around my neck:
Soon, this too
will be over.

The night,
a stripe through
the curtain. Stars,
a pale pinstripe
of light . . .

and somewhere,
somewhere out there,
the moon.
Where once I rode
sidesaddle, fast
before the shadow.
Where you, shepherd
Endymion, sleep
eternal, hollow
in a twisted sheet.
My shining cloak
in the closet, hung
next to your crook.

The last child of fifty,
finally, asleep.

Piano Wise

Joe, the piano man,
wrings a tune, mournful,
from the old cherrywood
upright. A London Chappell,
my father's father's
piano; he died
half a century ago.
In the will, the piano to me,
his infant granddaughter.
The importance of this relic
is implicit; my care of it, suspect.
The felt is worn from hammers,
strings rusted, pin blocks loose—
the whole thing
woefully neglected.

The story goes,
this piano came overseas
via my great uncle so-and-so—
a condition of his employment
by Coaker. There was no room
in the hold; it came on the deck,
tied to the mainmast;
uncrated, and played
as they sailed into port,
the notes ringing out
over the harbour.
This journey, it survived.
Its sojourn in my
living room, the enthusiastic
pumping of the sostenuto
and damper pedals
by the great-grandchildren,
it has not.

The wood still gleams
behind the scratches
and water stains,
but the keys are a mouthful
of misused teeth—
in the manner of the elderly,
cracked, and chipped,
the odd few
altogether missing.
Dust gathers in the chamfers;
the dovetails and dowelling rattle.
Nobody plays the thing
but we tune it religiously
for Christmas.

Dark clouds gather.
The whorled Schreger
lines of the remaining ivory
keytops recall fingerprints.
The ebonies are still sharp
as my father's fingertips
gripping a piece of chalk
in his basement office
or pinching a Player's
Filter while listening
to Rachmaninoff.
Of course, it's the naturals
that show their age.
Now the colour of an old man's
fingernails, they are slowly
yellowing outward from
middle C.

Joe, the piano man,
says: *Milk, but not much.*
Baking soda, just a touch
and begins a twinkling phrase
that, under his nimble
fingers, sounds like stars
in a bright sky or
the clear tinkle of glass;
ice, minutely shifting.
The heavy-bellied clouds
outside finally boil over.
Rain in ropes, a chaotic
counterpoint, batters
at the darkened windows.
Joe goes back to tapping
and plucking.
Harmonies converge,
saturate the air.

Wavering, wandering,
Joe picks out
each endless, tuneless
note to echo against
a more tuneful fraternal twin—
parents and grandparents
bow down dolefully,
siblings, children, and cousins
stretch up, anxiously.
Barely harmonious,
they drift, now together, ·
now apart; eventually
between them, resolving true,

a tenuous accord.
I see Joe to the door,
en route to tune another
heirloom for the holidays.
Over his shoulder,
into the howling weather,
he cracks wise.
Don't breathe too hard,
he says,
and is gone.

vi.

What We Do Not Know

A young man
is crying. Howling,
he has fallen
with one hand clinging
to the door handle
of my neighbor's car,
clutching some woman's
legs with the other.

She helps him up,
manhandling him
somehow. Hanging on
to one another, they make
their way awkwardly,
awfully, down the alleyway
to Colin's door.

Come to think of it,
I haven't seen Colin
for a few days,
maybe a week or more.

It's hard to know
when you have
small kids,
when you only
pass the time of day,
when he is just an older man
in a captain's hat,
out for his daily
stroll to the store
for beer.

We all know
Colin is an alcoholic,
but kind and pleased
to see the kids
in the neighborhood
out making a racket.

We all know
that the young man
(looking hard done by
and rumour has it,
homeless) comes by
on the regular to sit
with Colin. Eat a meal,
drink some beers,
talk philosophy.

Through my open window,
I hear him beg
for a cigarette.

What we do not know
yet—
the young man
had gone to Labrador
to bury his brother
who choked on
his own vomit.

What we do not know
yet—
Colin was his first
stop after that
terrible trip.

The young man
opened the door.
He called out for Colin.
It was dark and quiet
and Colin was lying
dead on the floor.

His face was purple.
He had been dead awhile.

The fire truck came first,
then ambulance, then police.

In they went
with equipment, came out again,
too fast,

and that first cop
had a real pale face
when he left.

Colin had been
looking real pale too, I guess.
But by the time
anyone noticed
he was gone.

The young man
came back, smoked
the cigarettes we gave him,
cried on the curb.
Hands shaking, said he was
hopeful. Colin had told him
many times—

he was an old man,
and if he died,
the thin house
in the alley
was his.

The young man
opened the windows,
to air it out from
the smell of dead Colin.
He cleaned the skinny house
that was built like a ship's galley.
But though he had no home
of his own, he would not sleep
there—not until
he was sure.

Then Colin's grim sister
came from somewhere
else and sold the place.
The young man drifted
away for good.

The girl
who lives there
now, in that hip, narrow
apartment, didn't know
Colin. That he died,
alone on her kitchen
floor. Lay there
for days.

That a young man
howled.

At Swim

(exeunt Graham Howcroft, stained glass artist)

The last gasp
of a cigarette,
the sluggish dregs
of drink—these
you left behind

for your backless
gown, your hospital
bed. Left it all
to the old, bitter
tribe, robed

in elderly velvet,
greying heads
bent beneath
the weight
of crooked crowns.

Your last court
was held, bereft
of your own gruff
voice. The ashes
of your body

inurned in the old
wooden church,
just down the road
from your house.
The boards there

creak underfoot
and corners
languish, unswept.
Storied panes
of jewelled glass

crack the light
blown breezeway
—your garden still
sparkles with
the discarded shards.

You,
finally,
at swim
in the
light.

Dark Hole River

There is a highway
beside the highway.

It begins where the
first black pond stands

still, beyond the edge
of the road. A shadow

street, deep beneath
twilight fog, caught

in the arms of over-
grown alders. An old

road, hove over by
rocks, where the broad

backs of glacial erratics,
barnacled by lichen, like

leviathan, breach the turf
like moss-backed whales.

Here is the tidal surge of
sod that will cover us all.

An arc of moonlight
emerges, reflecting in

black ponds, under black
ponds. Snarled by moose-

rubbed rock; sunk deep,
peat sleek in Labrador

tea; steeped in the blue,
crow, and partridgeberry,

a dark river, hidden
in every tangled path,

under each lane lost,
over all trails walked,

through every drung,
forgot. Run once by

moccasin and fox,
by shrew and vole,

that river is dark and
swift. There, coyotes

howl, where wolves
once bit that mighty

ghost, the storm
white caribou.

There is a highway
beside the highway.

In a sea
of black lakes.

In the land
of black rocks.

That, in the
darkness, we

miss.

Visitation

Through sheers, the sky,
cere-blue; flat-stitched
by herringbone cirrus.
Dawn, when tidewater comes seeping,
black under the back door.

I call out,
What do we do?!
Uselessly gathering shoes
and lifting books from the wet, you say,
Turn the breakers off!

The wind is blowing cold.
Our youngest out the side
door, on the hill.
A grey cat that was sleeping
yesterday, on a stone
in the sun, is dead.

I say to someone I can't
see, *Is that cat dead?*
And someone that isn't you

replies, *Well, something around here is.*
I think it's in there,

where a hole is in the hill.
I know something has crept
in deep and died because we see
the brown-straw hill swarm,
a burial mound braided
with jewel-tone flies—our child

picks up the sleeping cat.
Stiff, hard as stone, and cold.
Flies in a clump spill
out the whiskered mouth—your mother
is there, in a nightdress
that's white

and you say,
I should have known all along
where we could've gone—
it was Mom's . . .

Then, we hear her—distant
on the phone upstairs, she is so scared.
I came up to the room to pray and Les was there.
What do I do?

They are shadows, now,
behind the curtained doors.
I remember how each
packed a suitcase at the wharf
with stones and beach rocks,
and one by one, walked off.

Now, that tide pulses
at our own back door,
and finally, the answer comes—
nothing and *no one.*

Glad and Leander, Albert, Margaret,
and Viola, too—Joyce in a twin-set,
outside laughing, like that old
milk cow never kicked her
and her bucket over.

Everyone that old, dark
water has ever closed over,
is seeping under every door
on our ground floor.
Each one bent
on coming back
home.

Notes

"Ornery Corner"

This poem references locations in the 1970s and '80s Rabbittown neighborhood of St. John's, where I grew up, including landmarks like Badcock's Fish Market, Merrymeeting Laundromat, and the Cottage Club, a neighborhood pub that rented rooms hourly and eventually burned down. The Umma Mumma Man was a name coined by neighborhood children for the local travelling shoeshine man. Johnny Gluebag was a character reputed to sniff glue; he was widely accused of stealing money from collection plates in churches, and universally blamed for any petty crime that occurred in the neighborhood. OZFM is a local rock radio station that began broadcasting in 1977. This poem was previously published in *Riddle Fence*, Volume 26, as "Aldershot n Summer."

"Oh Wanda Whalen"

The line "Who are you … Who are you?" refers to the title of the song "Who Are You," written by The Who in 1978.

"Re: Muskrat Falls"

The Newfoundland and Labrador cod moratorium was announced on July 2, 1992, effectively obliterating the income, industry, traditions, and cultural landscape of the province. In the years following, the federal government was accused of turning a blind eye to international commercial interests that routinely crossed the 200-mile limit to harvest fish stocks from an area regulated and heavily enforced for Newfoundland and Labrador fishers. The *Estai* was a fishing trawler from Galicia, eventually apprehended by the Canadian Fisheries Patrol and RCMP for taking undersized fish on the Grand Banks and forced to port in St. John's harbour, where a performative political media scrum took place as the Spanish fishers (pescadores) disembarked. Restrictions on the NL commercial and food fisheries continue to this day.

Muskrat Falls is a hydroelectric project by NL Crown corporation Nalcor Energy, begun in 2013. Nalcor pushed forward with the damming of the Lower

Churchill River, despite concerns about methylmercury flowing downstream and contaminating the drinking water and food sources of Inuit and other communities. Widespread protests followed. The 2017 Muskrat Falls Inquiry revealed corruption, a budget nearly doubled, and long delays. Nalcor has since been absorbed by Newfoundland and Labrador Hydro, another Crown corporation. The Muskrat Falls hydroelectric project continues to be plagued by mechanical issues, methylmercury concerns, projected steep costs for taxpayers, and is still not fully operational as of 2023.

"Last Hours, in Port," "Last Hours, at Sea," and "Last Hours, on Stage"

The MV *Lyubov Orlova* was a luxury Arctic cruise liner built in Yugoslavia in 1976. She was named after a famous and troubled Russian stage and movie star (Lyubov Petrovna Orlova, 1902–1975) who was championed by Joseph Stalin in the 1930s. The vessel was taken out of service in 2010 and abandoned at St. John's Harbour for several years, where she became derelict and overrun by rats. In early 2013, she broke her towline enroute to the Dominican Republic to be sold for scrap. The Canadian government eventually managed to recapture the vessel, towed her to international waters, and set her adrift. Popularly known as the "Cannibal Rat Ghost Ship," the *Orlova* captured international interest as she drifted the North Atlantic for several months, sending out occasional distress beacons. She was never found and is assumed to have sunk somewhere off the coast of Ireland in the spring of 2013.

The poem "Last Hours, at Sea" features a series of repeating dots and dashes. These represent the Morse code for SOS.

"Goodnight Moon"

The title of this poem references the famous and beloved 1947 children's book of the same name by Margaret Wise Brown (1910–1952). Brown was considered revolutionary in her bold, intuitive, and simplistic approach to children's literature, and she wrote dozens of books, often featuring animal characters and elements of the natural world. Brown engaged in a tumultuous long-term relationship with heiress Blanche Oelrichs (1890–1950), a writer and performer who went by the name Michael Strange. Late in their relationship, Michael contracted leukemia and became quite ill, eventually embracing religion, and ultimately rejecting Brown in the time leading up to her death. Brown was devastated and died suddenly of natural causes two years later.

"Titans"

This poem was inspired by the loss of the *Titan* submersible in June 2023, near the *Titanic* wreck, deep in the North Atlantic Ocean, off the coast of Newfoundland and Labrador.

"Atwood Machine"

The Atwood Machine is a piece of lab equipment invented in 1784 by English mathematician George Atwood. It is used for the purposes of verifying the mechanical laws of motion, by way of constant acceleration.

The Fibonacci series (0, 1, 1, 2, 3, 5, 6, 13 . . .) is a mathematical sequence conceived by Italian mathematician Leonardo Fibonacci in the early 1200s. He used the sequence to solve a problem concerning population growth among rabbits. Each number in the sequence is the sum of the two previous numbers. The Fibonacci series is also closely associated with the Golden Ratio in visual art, the natural world, and also in chaos theory.

In this poem, "Higgsian" refers to the Higgs boson, a quantum particle (sometimes referred to as "the God particle") predicted by Peter Higgs in the 1960s and discovered by Higgs and François Englert in 2012 in the CERN Large Hadron Collider. The Higgs boson is closely associated with the Higgs field, which confers mass to all components that make up our universe. There is only a one in one billion chance of a Higgs boson appearing and being detected in a particle collider.

Henri Poincaré was a French mathematician, theoretical physicist, engineer, and scientific philosopher in the late nineteenth century. His work in various disciplines, particularly in theoretical topography, laid the foundations for modern chaos theory.

Chaotic lace and regular dust sets are components of complex dynamics: a branch of mathematics. The Julia set consists of values that may change drastically in response to minimal stimulation (thus, chaotic) while the Fatou set is more regular and stable (hence, a more even "dust settling" pattern). These are based on the early twentieth century work of French mathematicians Gaston Julia and Pierre Fatou.

Both the Noah and Joseph effects were developed by Benoit Mandelbrot, a Polish-born French American mathematician, in the twentieth century. The Noah effect is chaotic and unpredictable, while the Joseph effect is both continuous and predictable.

The free fall apparatus is a piece of lab equipment used to demonstrate the motion of a body in free fall.

The double pendulum is a simple experiment consisting of two pendulums attached end-to-end. Once set in motion, the oscillations of this mechanism are very sensitive to even slight external stimuli and respond unpredictably, with vastly different outcomes that are difficult to describe mathematically. The double pendulum experiment is often used to illustrate problems in chaos theory and was invented in 1655 by the Dutch astronomer Christiaan Huygens.

"The Hours it Takes"

This poem was previously published in *Riddle Fence*, Volume 26, as "IV (for Ivy)."

"Spring Is in the Gut"

In this poem, the "gut" carries a dual meaning, referring to both the anatomical region of the body and the geographic location, Quidi Vidi Gut, in St. John's, which flows from Quidi Vidi Lake into the North Atlantic Ocean. When walking the trail around the lake, you will also encounter the Canadian Forces Garrison in Pleasantville (the home of the Royal Newfoundland Regiment Band, the brass band in this poem), Country Ribbon Inc. (a chicken processing plant), Her Majesty's Penitentiary (a crumbling prison that dates back to Victorian times), and the tree-filled Forest Road Anglican Cemetery, which has been in use since the 1840s.

"Celestial Bodies"

This poem was previously published in *Riddle Fence*, Volume 46, as "Blood Moon Boys."

"Selene Sees the Moon"

Selene is the Greek goddess of the Moon who is often pictured riding a horse or driving a chariot across the night sky. She is reputed to have had 50 daughters by her lover, the mortal shepherd Endymion, who was cursed with eternal sleep by Zeus. As mother to four of my own children, I find the mythos of Selene intriguing.

"Piano Wise"

Piano Wise Inc. is the name of a piano tuning business in St. John's, owned and operated by Joe Tompkins. This poem was inspired by a visit from Joe to tune our elderly upright piano. Schreger lines are the faint, fingerprint-like patterns that are visible in natural ivory. The expertise of Piano Wise Inc., for piano tuning, service, and repair, may be arranged by calling 709-745-8127 in St. John's and surrounding areas.

Acknowledgements

I wrote the poems in this collection over the course of about ten years, assembling them from scraps of paper, half-remembered dreams, napkins, and the backs of grocery receipts, while deep in the trenches of parenting four young children. I am deeply grateful for the inspiration, support, and love of my steadfast partner Barry and the four shining stars of our lives—Max, Charlie, Rudy, and Ivy—I love you all with the heat of a thousand blazing suns! Thank you to my parents, Maynard and Eleanor Clouter, for encouraging my love of words from a young age. Blessings to my teachers, mentors, and fellow writers for inspiration, and also to anyone who has ever invited me to join a writing group, offered to babysit, hectored me to submit a piece of writing, brought me a coffee, a drink, a shoulder to cry on, or supplied me with a quiet corner to write in. Lastly, deep gratitude to everyone at Riddle Fence for putting their confidence in this "late in life" debut author, and especially to my editor, Sue Goyette, for helping me understand what this collection was trying to say.

Jennifer May Newhook is an award-winning writer with current practice in short- and long-form narrative fiction, dramatic script, and poetry. Her work appears in literary journals and publications nationally and internationally. She has recently completed her first novel, *The Gulch*, and is currently researching the second, *Maggot Beach*. Jennifer lives in downtown St. John's, NL (Ktaqmkuk) with her partner and four children.